Contents

Introduction

Advances in communications **technology** this century have brought about real changes in our everyday lives. Thanks to modern **telecommunications**, we can pick up a telephone and talk to other people almost anywhere in the world. A system called facsimile transmission, or fax, enables us to send pictures, drawings and printed text by telephone. Videoconferencing allows people to have face-to-face meetings without having to be in the same room or even in the same country. Spacecraft tens of thousands of kilometres above us constantly observe the Earth and send back valuable information that often could not be collected at ground level.

Computers in different parts of the world can exchange **data**, relaying information on business and financial matters to organizations within seconds. This enables businesses and governments to react quickly to rapidly changing situations. Combining computers and telecommunications is called information technology, or IT. Photography, cinema and broadcasting are all forms of communication too. They all allow information and ideas collected in one place to be stored and transported to different places.

Advances in communications are beginning to affect the way people work and where they work. People who work mainly with information can work at home, exchanging information by telephone, fax and post. This is called teleworking or telecommuting. The author of this book is a teleworker.

The key to the future growth in communications is the development of the Integrated Services **Digital Network** (ISDN). This enables all sorts of information, ranging from conversations to computer data, to be transmitted along the same information pathways. Most developed countries now have an ISDN. It provides more services more reliably than the old **analogue** telephone system.

Communications in the Third World

That paints a very rosy picture of the state of communications technology and what it can do for people in developed countries such as the United States. But almost four fifths of the world's population live in developing countries where most people do not have access to these advanced systems. A developing country often has large numbers of people working in the countryside where transport, power supplies, technical assistance and communications are all in short supply. It is now recognized that good communications are vital to the development of these countries.

This book examines communications in its many forms and looks forward to some of the developments that we can expect to see in years to come. Issues that you might like to think about for yourself are featured in **Data for discussion** boxes. Words in bold type in the text are explained at the end of each section.

Computers at the control centre (right) of one American telephone company select the best routes for long distance calls.
A new telephone exchange is being delivered in Kenya (bottom right). Telephone systems in developing countries are far behind those in the First World.
Olympus class communications satellites (below) will eventually handle telephone, radio and television signals.

technology — the application of science to solving practical problems.

telecommunications — communications by means of telephone, radio or television.

data — information, especially information in a form that can be processed by a computer.

digital — a digital signal consists of a stream of electrical pulses, all the same size. The pattern, or code, of the pulses carries the information.

network — a system of equipment such as radio sets, telephones or computers connected to each other so that they can communicate with each other.

analogue — an analogue signal is an electrical copy of the original information. An analogue telephone line carries an electrical signal that varies in step with the voice. Compare this to **digital**.

In the home

In the 1990s and beyond, more television sets, video recorders, hi-fi systems and even household appliances such as washing machines will be able to communicate with each other and with their owners. In 1989 two companies, Philips in Europe and Matsushita in Japan, announced that they had jointly developed a standard code or 'language' for controlling machines in the home, called D^2B. D^2B stands for Domestic Digital **Bus**. D^2B signals can be transmitted around a house in several ways – by **fibre optic cable, infra-red beams** and radio signals – and through the mains electrical circuit.

Machines take over

The Domestic Digital Bus should make homes easier to manage, and appliances easier to use. For example, when a new television set is brought into a house, it normally has to be programmed with all the available television channels. In some countries where dozens of channels can be received, this can take a long time. If the television set 'understands' the D^2B code and if a D^2B video recorder is already in the house, the television channel numbers can simply be transferred from the video recorder's memory to the new television set along a cable connecting the two together. D^2B should also cut out the need for instruction manuals that tell you how to operate machines. The instructions for using a new washing machine, for example, will be programmed into microchips inside the

The media room. The appearance of the living room (inset) is gradually changing as home entertainment systems develop. In a computerized house in Dallas, USA (main picture), a whole wall is filled with audiovisual equipment.

HOUSEWORK BY REMOTE CONTROL

In the future, it will be possible to operate household machines from a distance, by telephone, and security systems will be much more effective. Some of the features of this automated house are already available, while others are being tested. (See also page 8.)

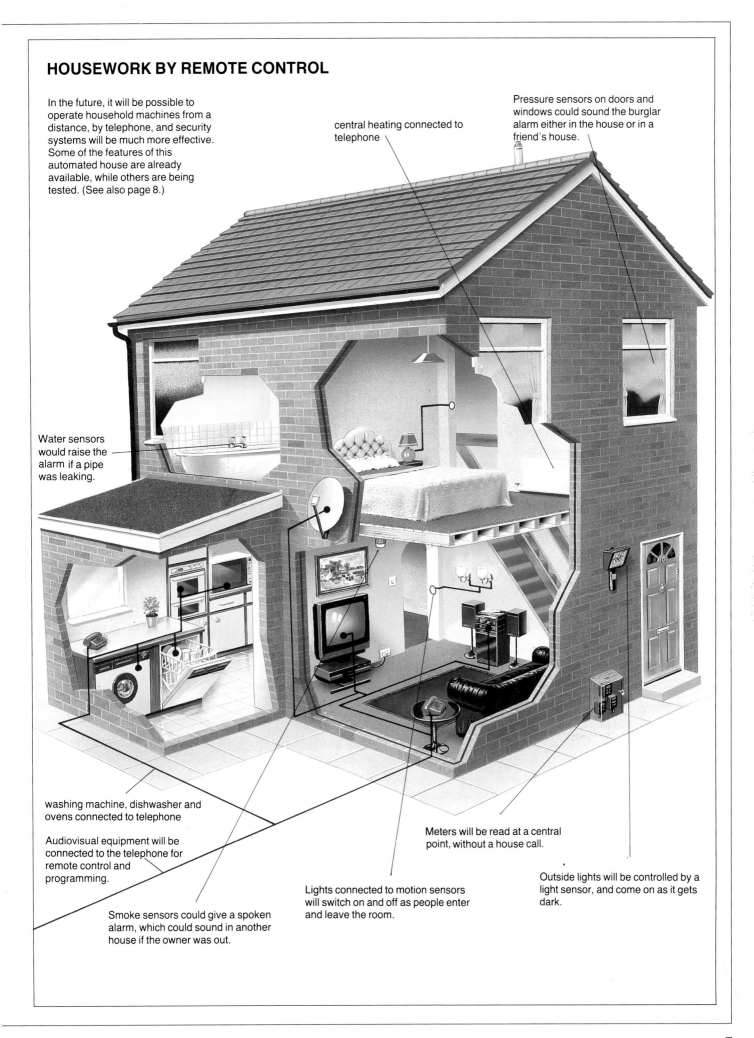

central heating connected to telephone

Pressure sensors on doors and windows could sound the burglar alarm either in the house or in a friend's house.

Water sensors would raise the alarm if a pipe was leaking.

washing machine, dishwasher and ovens connected to telephone

Audiovisual equipment will be connected to the telephone for remote control and programming.

Smoke sensors could give a spoken alarm, which could sound in another house if the owner was out.

Meters will be read at a central point, without a house call.

Lights connected to motion sensors will switch on and off as people enter and leave the room.

Outside lights will be controlled by a light sensor, and come on as it gets dark.

machine. By pressing buttons on the machine's remote control handset, you will cause the instructions to be displayed on a television screen.

If appliances such as refrigerators are manufactured to D^2B standards, they may be able to alert the owner to faults and problems. For example, if the door of a refrigerator is left open, the fridge may be able to detect this and warn the owner by flashing a message on the television screen.

Turning off the light

D^2B is only the first step in a grander plan. Further in the future, it will lead to more automatic equipment and appliances in homes. For example, after dark, sensors will detect the heat and movement of a person entering a room and switch on the lights automatically. When the last person leaves the room, the lights will be switched off again automatically. This will save energy, as the tiny amount of electrical power used by the sensors would be more than matched by the saving in not having lights on unnecessarily in empty rooms.

Safety and security

Later developments of the same system will help to make homes more safe and secure. Smoke sensors will be linked into the system. If smoke is detected in the house, a warning could be flashed on to the television screen. Alternatively, a voice created by a computer could speak a warning. If an intruder enters the house without operating the door locks correctly, detectors will sense the intruder's presence in the house and sound an alarm.

The home control system will be connected to the telephone, so that any member of the household can operate equipment from a distance. If you are going to be late home from work, you will be able to telephone the house and programme the video recorder, turn on the oven and the lights, and so on. Being able to control the house by telephone will create security problems. Security codes, or **passwords**, will have to be used to prevent unauthorized people from telephoning a house and interfering with its control system. Some organizations will have access to the automated home. Electricity meters will be read by sending information from them through the mains wiring to the electricity supply company. Gas and water meters could be read in the same way. Meter reading through the mains is already being tried out in an experiment in London.

All these projects depend on a system that allows communication between different pieces of equipment. The system can only work if all the equipment being used understands the same standard code for instructions and information.

Design detail

Designers of home automation, control and security systems face one particularly difficult problem that is not experienced by designers of individual products. A successful home control system must be able to cope with changing technology in the home. Its designers have to look into the future and try to predict how home technology will develop, so that their control system is made as 'future proof' as possible. This involves lengthy discussions with the manufacturers of everything from dishwashers to

In an automated house the computer screen (far left) would be used to check the heating, lighting, ventilation and security. The systems would be controlled from a control panel (left) in the house, or by telephone.

satellite television receivers, so that everyone agrees on how the control system will work and to ensure that all the products made by manufacturers in different countries can be linked to the system.

Video games

In the 1990s, home entertainment will change dramatically. Video games, for example, will benefit from advances in computer and communications technology. The storage capacity of computers doubles every three or four years. The computer graphics used in the latest video games take up a lot of memory. The bigger a computer's storage capacity is, the more complicated are the graphics that it can produce. In the next decade we should see more lifelike three-dimensional (3-D) graphics in games. Video games will also be able to mix recordings of the real world with computer graphics and soundtracks of music, voices and

Video games played on a computer screen (top right) will soon be replaced by more complex and lifelike systems. In 'virtual reality' computer systems, players wear a helmet (bottom right) fitted with tiny television screens which create 3-D images. Players feel as if they are in another world. In sit-down versions (above) they might, for example, fly a plane or drive a car.

special effects. This newly developing technology is known as multimedia. Manufacturers of multimedia equipment estimate that the world market for their business and leisure products will be worth over 24,000 million dollars by 1994. By the end of the 1990s, it is possible that multimedia video games will have evolved into the home control and automation systems described on page 6.

Fact or fiction?

The most exciting development in games playing is the 'virtual reality' game, which is based on computer research for military and Space use (see pages 9 and 35). The player wears a special helmet with a visor in front of his or her eyes. The computer creates an artificial world and projects it on to the player's visor. If the player turns his or her head, the computer detects this and changes the picture on the visor. In more advanced versions of the game, if the player reaches out for anything in the picture, a computer-created hand appears in the picture, matching the position of the player's hand. The player feels as if he or she really is in the world created by the computer.

Laser games

Laser discs are increasingly popular as a means of storing the computer data that is used to display games on a television screen. When used for this purpose, the discs are referred to as **CD-ROMs** (Compact Disc Read-Only Memory). The system's ability to jump to any part of the disc within a fraction of a second and display different parts of the game in a different order each time it is played is ideal for computer games.

The CD-ROM can hold enormous amounts of information. Magnetic discs commonly used to store computer data each hold almost three quarters of a million letters, numbers or other symbols. A CD-ROM can hold almost 1,000 times that amount of data and any piece of information on the disc can be reached and read within a second. The next generation of games, with 3-D graphics and the ability to react in very complicated ways to the player's actions, will need the CD-ROM's incredible storage capacity.

Learning from laser discs

Laser discs store sound, pictures and computer data as a pattern of microscopic pits etched into the disc's surface. When the disc is loaded into a player, it is spun at high speed and a laser beam is focused on it from underneath. The beam is reflected from the disc's mirror-like surface into a light-sensitive cell, which produces an electric current. The pits in the disc's surface are not reflective. When the laser beam strikes a pit, little or no light is reflected and the electrical signal from the cell falls. The signal from the cell is converted from a series of pulses back into copies of the original music or pictures that gave rise to the code.

The laser can be moved to read the data at any part of a laser disc within a second. This is called 'random access' and it makes laser discs perfect for education. A series of lessons can be recorded on a laser disc. During each lesson, the student is asked questions and has to respond by pressing buttons on a control panel or a computer keyboard. Depending on how well the student answers, the computer chooses which lesson the student should do next. This is called interactive video and it is used extensively in education and training in industry. In future, courses on foreign languages and other subjects could be put on laser disc for home use.

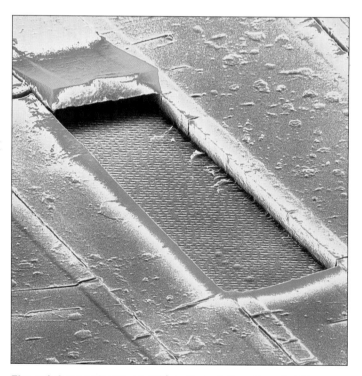

The rainbow colours on this compact disc (top right) are produced as light falls on the microscopic pits on the disc. In this magnified view (above) the plastic coating which protects the disc from dust and scratches has been peeled away to show the pattern of pits. Each pit is only half of a thousandth of a millimetre deep.

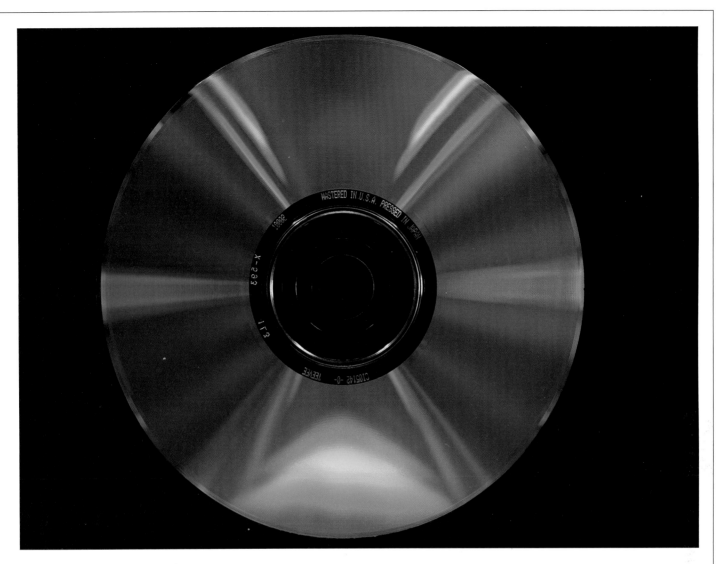

LASERS AT WORK

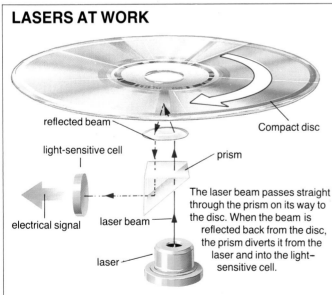

reflected beam

light-sensitive cell

electrical signal

laser beam

laser

prism

Compact disc

The laser beam passes straight through the prism on its way to the disc. When the beam is reflected back from the disc, the prism diverts it from the laser and into the light-sensitive cell.

Data for discussion

• Would you like to live in a house controlled by D^2B? What would be some of the advantages and disadvantages?

bus – in electronics, a bus is a pathway for information.

fibre optic cable – a cable made from a bundle of fine glass strands. Information is sent along the cable as an intense beam of light.

infra-red beams – invisible energy that lies between visible light and radio waves, just beyond the red end of the rainbow. Hot objects give out more infra-red energy than cool objects.

passwords – words (or numbers) known only to people who are allowed to operate a system. The system will not operate until it receives the correct passwords.

CD-ROM – Compact Disc Read-Only Memory. This is a laser disc used to store computer data instead of music. The data cannot be erased and new data recorded in its place. It is therefore a 'read only' device for storing information.

Making a telephone call

Alexander Graham Bell (above), a Scots-born American scientist, invented the telephone in 1876.

The telephone was invented over 100 years ago, but it is still the most important communications device in the home and in business. It is taken for granted today that a caller can speak to someone on the other side of the world just by dialling a telephone number. But how does the system work?

Getting through

When a caller somewhere in the UK, for example, dials a number in the USA, the call is routed by copper cable to a local telephone exchange. From there, perhaps by **optical fibre**, it goes to an international exchange. From there, it travels to a satellite Earth station. It may get there by cable, optical fibre or microwave radio signals. A huge dish-shaped aerial, up to 30 metres across, transmits the call to a communications satellite over the Atlantic Ocean. This receives the call and re-transmits it down to another Earth station in the USA, from where the call is routed through the US telephone system to its destination. When the person receiving the call speaks, his or her words make the reverse journey back to Britain.

New for old. This mass of copper wires (above) can be replaced by the optical fibre cable (right).

Using light

Traditional copper cables are being replaced by cables made from fine strands of glass called optical fibres. A single glass fibre can carry over 2,000 telephone conversations, all going on at the same time, but not interfering with each other. A bundle of fibres capable of carrying 100,000 telephone calls would be thin enough to pass through the eye of a needle. An equivalent copper cable would be 10 times as thick. Telephone calls are carried along an optical cable as pulses of light. The way the fibre is made ensures that light travels along its length without escaping. The glass used to make optical fibres is so pure that a block of it 20 kilometres thick would be as clear as a window pane.

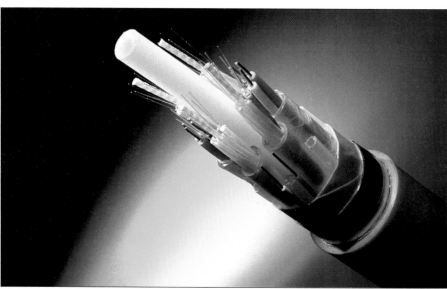

EN ROUTE FROM THE UK TO THE USA

A telephone call from a home or office in the UK passes along a copper cable to the local exchange, then along fibre optic cable to an international exchange (1). Calls from in or near London then pass through the Telecom Tower in London (2), which can handle 172,000 calls at once. Fibre optic cable carries it to a microwave relay tower (3), sited on high ground, which sends it to the satellite Earth station (4). From there it is beamed up to the satellite (5), and then retransmitted along a similar route back to Earth.

5

4

3

2

1

Phones for the future

Microelectronics, computer technology and **satellites** have made the telephone system more reliable and more useful in recent years, but some of the biggest changes still await us in the near future. The telephone of the 1990s will be smaller, lighter and cordless. It will be connected to the telephone network by radio.

In future it will be much easier to make a phone call than it is now. Telephones will not only be able to store more telephone numbers in their memory and dial them automatically, but they will also be able to understand human speech. Some telephones can already understand a few words. One telephone now available in the USA can store up to 150 telephone numbers in its memory and it will dial up to 50 of them when it hears a spoken command. The name and number of the person being dialled is displayed on a small screen on the telephone.

A new radio-telephone service will make it easier to make telephone calls from ships at sea. They used to be made by first contacting a telephone operator by radio and asking for the number to be dialled. The new system will allow calls to be made to anywhere in the world by dialling the number directly from the ship, just as if it were being made from a normal telephone on land. The ship must be within radio range of a country with the equipment needed to decode the dialling signal from the ship and route the call through to the telephone network. Since the equipment has been standardized throughout the world, the system should work anywhere as long as enough countries install the equipment that is needed on land.

Telephone links in China are about 20 years behind those in developed countries, but communications are being given priority in major cities.

In-flight phone calls

Similar systems will also enable airline passengers to make telephone calls. Experimental systems are already being used. The first European phone-in-flight service, Skyphone, was started by British Airways on its transatlantic flights in 1989. Calls are relayed from the aircraft to receiving stations on the ground via a satellite positioned in orbit over the Atlantic Ocean.

A call from above (left). Airline passengers will soon be able to make telephone calls and send faxes during a flight.

Telecommunications are important in a country such as Brazil (far left), where the population is spread over a wide area.

Phones on the move

A new type of telephone, called a personal communicator, will be introduced in the 1990s. The personal communicator is designed as a telephone for the person instead of for a place. It can be used as a mobile car phone, a cordless portable phone, a desk-top office phone and a home phone. It can be carried everywhere and will be small enough and light enough to slip into a pocket. People who own these new phones will keep the same number for ever, wherever they live or move to.

Data for discussion
● It is possible to make telephones that show the caller's telephone number before you answer the phone. How might this be useful?

optical fibre– a fine strand of glass.
satellites – unmanned spacecraft in orbit around a planet.

The telephone of the future – the personal communicator – will fit into a pocket.

Music on the line

Telephone sound quality is generally rather poor. It is certainly not up to hi-fi music standards. However, if the music could be sent as a digital signal (see page 5), the sound quality would be much better. Unfortunately, the digital code that represents a piece of music also contains more information than a conventional telephone line can handle. By using the most advanced code compression techniques, developed at Queen's University, Belfast, the amount of information can be reduced to the point where CD-quality music can be transmitted by telephone. In future, it may be possible to telephone a music library and receive a selection of music. The music could be recorded and used later for a party or to play on a long car journey.

Big business

The telephone can do far more than simply letting people talk to each other. Computer data, printed text, drawings, photographs, moving video pictures and even **CD**-quality music can be transmitted by telephone (see page 15). The systems that made these facilities possible were developed for business use, but as the cost of the equipment has fallen, smaller businesses and even private individuals have started using them.

Sending printed messages

The need for printed messages to be exchanged between businesses led to the development of the telex service. The old telex service, dating from the 1930s, is still used by so many businesses that it will be many years before it is phased out. Electronic mail (E-mail) and facsimile transmission (fax) are now replacing telex. Electronic mail enables messages to be sent from one computer to another. The two computers could be in different streets, towns or countries. As long as they are linked to telephones, it does not matter where they are.

The advantage of E-mail is that a printed message can be sent from one office computer to another on the other side of the world within seconds. The message could take days or weeks to make the same journey by post.

Fax machines can send printed text, drawings and photographs by telephone. As the pages are fed into the fax machine, an intense light shines on the paper. The paper reflects the light on to a light-sensitive sensor. This converts whatever is printed on the paper into an electrical signal, and this is transmitted by telephone. The receiving fax machine converts the coded signal back into a copy of the original document and prints it on paper stored in the machine. New uses for fax machines are being found all the time, including 'electronic newspapers'. (See page 27.)

Seeing is believing

Science fiction writers have often featured telephones with video screens in their stories, but videophones have proved to be more difficult to design in real life. Moving pictures are difficult to transmit by telephone because they contain more information than the telephone line can carry. One experimental videophone link, set up between Los Angeles and New York in 1956 by the Bell Telephone Company, occupied the equivalent of 125 telephone lines and was soon abandoned as impractical.

The videophone has been revived recently, thanks to digital electronics. This has made it possible to turn a video picture into a digital code and then reduce the amount of information that has to be transmitted by a process called digital compression. Videophones are now on sale in several countries, including Japan and Britain. When **ISDN** services are more widely available later in the 1990s, they will enable videophone signals to be transmitted more easily and videophones should become more popular.

A videoconference link-up (top right) allows people to 'meet' without wasting time and money travelling to one place.
In the year 2000, fax machines (below) may be as common in homes as video recorders are now.
The videophone (bottom right) allows telephone users to see each other.

Business meetings

Some people spend a great deal of time in planes, trains and cars travelling to and from business meetings. This is not only costly, it also wastes time that could be spent doing useful work. For some companies, the answer is the videoconference. People who want to meet go to

their local videoconference centres. Each centre is a room fitted with a conference table and chairs and a row of television screens. The screens show people in other centres. Cameras and microphones transmit the pictures and sound of people in each centre to all the other centres that are taking part in the conference. Large companies might install their own video-conference centre in their own office building.

ISDN will make videoconferences much easier and less expensive to set up in the future. People will be able to use the videophones on their desks for videoconferences, by linking several videophones together temporarily.

Data for discussion
● A videophone shows telephone callers a live picture of each other. Do you think this is a good idea?

CD – Compact Disc. A mirror-like disc used for making high-quality recordings of music.
ISDN – Integrated Services Digital Network. (See page 4.)

Satellites in Space

The first communications satellite, Telstar, was launched in 1962. The 90-centimetre sphere could relay 60 telephone calls across the Atlantic Ocean. Its low orbit meant that it could only be contacted from both sides of the Atlantic for up to 20 minutes at a time before it passed overhead and out of range. Today, communications satellites – comsats – can relay over 40,000 telephone calls and three television channels simultaneously, and they are never out of range of their ground stations.

Comsats are now placed in a special orbit called a geostationary orbit 36,000 kilometres above the equator. Satellites in this orbit circle the Earth once every 24 hours, so that they appear to be stationary above the same point on the Earth's surface. Comsats have become much bigger over the years as more powerful launch rockets have been developed to place them in orbit. The largest commercial comsats weigh over two tonnes. They are the satellites that form the US Tracking and Data Relay Satellite System (TDRSS). The network relays communications signals between satellites in low orbits and their ground control stations on Earth. The US Space agency **NASA** also uses the TDRSS for communications with its Space shuttles. The satellite or Space shuttle transmits upwards to the nearest TDRS, which then relays the signals around the satellite network until one of the satellites is in contact with the ground control centre. The signals are then transmitted down to it.

The Space shuttle was used to place the Tracking and Data Relay Satellites in orbit.

Satellites to the rescue

Satellite communications – satcoms – are becoming increasingly important in the rescue operations that follow natural disasters such as floods and earthquakes. The countries that are affected most by these natural disasters also tend to be countries with poor communications networks. In any case, telephone lines, roads and other links with the rest of the world are often damaged by the disaster. Rescue teams

need efficient communications if they are to help people quickly. So now they often use mobile satcoms terminals (a telephone linked by cable to a small satellite dish) to stay in contact with their bases.

Mobile satcoms terminals are also used by survey teams working in remote areas looking for mineral and oil reserves. Another important use for mobile satcoms is in keeping a check on the numbers of trees that are being cut down in rainforests. These forests absorb carbon dioxide gas from the air and give out oxygen, the gas that we need to breathe. As trees are cut down, the amount of carbon dioxide in the air increases. The carbon dioxide traps more of the Sun's heat near the Earth, which warms up. This is called the greenhouse effect. If the Earth warms up too much, it could have a disastrous effect on our weather and cause the sea level to rise, flooding coastal cities. It is important, therefore, to monitor the forests. Mobile satcoms enable forestry officials to guide the police directly to problem areas to deal with illegal forest clearance. (See also page 39.)

Calling for help. Communications are often destroyed by floods (top left, in the USA) and earthquakes (above, in Mexico). Following disasters, and in remote areas (below, in Scotland) rescue teams rely heavily on mobile satellite communications equipment to keep in touch with their bases.

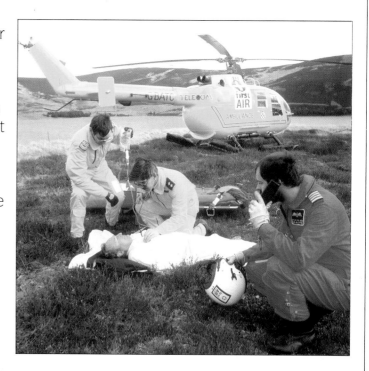

On the road: truck talk

In future, many of the trucks that transport goods by road across countries and continents will make use of satellite communications. Truck drivers will be able to talk to their bases at any time. (Mobile phones and CB radio only provide contact over a short range.) In the USA almost 10,000 trucks were fitted with satellite communications equipment in 1989 alone. Europe will begin to catch up with the USA during the 1990s.

The cost of installing a satcoms system will soon be recovered. Empty trucks lose money. Satcoms mean that the driver of an empty or part-filled truck can be asked to change his route to pick up a load. Satcoms can also provide a way of automatically monitoring a truck's progress. Systems that will become available in the 1990s will be able to show a truck's position to within a few metres. If a truck gets into difficulties, the driver can also use the system to call for assistance.

Mobile satcoms terminals also have an important role to play in medical assistance to the Third World (see photograph).

Doctors in the Third World (above) can use mobile satcoms terminals to relay images of patients to specialists in other countries. The patient does not have to travel long distances for a diagnosis, so treatment can be started quickly.

Working at sea. An oil rig in sight of land can use microwave radio to keep in touch with people on the land. Over long distances contact can still be made without satellites by bouncing radio waves off a layer of the atmosphere called the troposphere. The aerials used are called tropospheric scatterers.

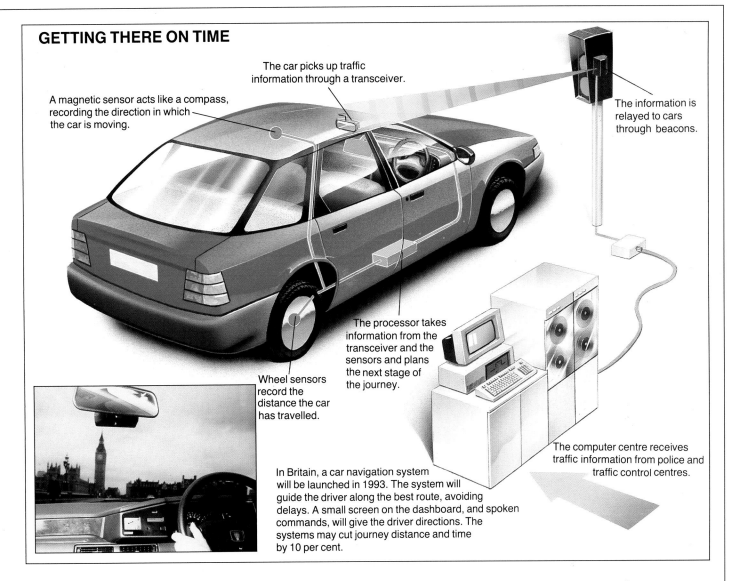

GETTING THERE ON TIME

A magnetic sensor acts like a compass, recording the direction in which the car is moving.

The car picks up traffic information through a transceiver.

The information is relayed to cars through beacons.

The processor takes information from the transceiver and the sensors and plans the next stage of the journey.

Wheel sensors record the distance the car has travelled.

The computer centre receives traffic information from police and traffic control centres.

In Britain, a car navigation system will be launched in 1993. The system will guide the driver along the best route, avoiding delays. A small screen on the dashboard, and spoken commands, will give the driver directions. The systems may cut journey distance and time by 10 per cent.

Finding the way

In future, more of us will be able to find out exactly where we are, and how to get to our destination, thanks to **navigation** satellites. The satellite end of the system, called the Global Positioning System (GPS), was first designed for use by US military forces. In 1990, Japan became the first country whose motorists could use the system. A total of 24 satellites orbit the Earth, each sending out continuous radio signals. Eight or nine satellites should be within radio contact of any point on Earth at any time. The receiver in the car needs to be able to contact at least four of them to calculate its position. The result is shown on a tiny television screen. A street map stored on a laser disc is first displayed on the screen and then the car's position, accurate to within 100 metres, is added. Some countries, including Britain, are concentrating on a different type of car navigation system. A receiver in the car takes information from roadside radio transmitters, or beacons. The disadvantage of this type of system is that a great many radio beacons are needed and they can be costly to keep in good working order.

Cars of the future will have a computer screen to give information on fuel consumption, engine performance, route, and even what is playing on the CD.

Astronomy in orbit

Satellites can often see things and do things in Space that cannot be seen or done at the Earth's surface. Astronomers measure the radiation from distant stars to find out how hot they are, what they are made from, and so on. But the Earth's **atmosphere** stops some of a star's radiation from reaching the Earth's surface, and it distorts some of the radiation that does get through. The best place for the instruments used to study the stars is in Space, above the Earth's atmosphere.

Many scientific instruments have been launched into Space in the past 30 years. Their size and weight was limited by the rockets available to launch them. The US Space shuttle has enabled scientists to place much larger instruments in orbit. The most important in the coming years will be the Hubble Space Telescope. The telescope, named after the US astronomer Edwin Hubble, is huge compared to the satellites that the Space shuttle normally launches. It is over 13 metres long, four metres across and it weighs 11 tonnes.

The Hubble Space Telescope is controlled by radio signals from Earth. The pictures of distant stars and galaxies taken by the telescope are sent down to Earth by radio. After the telescope was launched, a fault was discovered in the shape of one of its mirrors, making it impossible to obtain sharp pictures. Scientists believe that this fault can be corrected by astronauts on shuttle flights later in the 1990s.

As we rely more and more on spacecraft for our communications, navigation and scientific research, Space communications will become more important. During the 1990s, the US Space agency NASA plans to start building a Space station in orbit round the Earth. Space shuttles will transport scientists to laboratories in the station where they will be able to carry out experiments. As the Space station system grows, a new Space communications system will grow with it.

> **NASA** – National Aeronautics and Space Administration. The USA's main aviation and Space research organization.
> **navigation** – finding a safe route from one place to another place, especially by ship or aircraft.
> **atmosphere** – the layer of gases that surrounds the Earth.

The Hubble Space Telescope, (right, inset, still attached to the Space Shuttle arm) was launched in 1990. Once released from the arm (still visible in the main picture, right), the solar panels, which power the telescope, opened out.

The Orion Nebula (below) is a cloud of gas and dust where stars are being born. Astronomers study it by measuring the radiation from it through a telescope. The photographs show the cloud in visible light (left), at radio wavelengths (centre) and at infrared wavelengths (right). A computer shows the different kinds of energy as different colours.

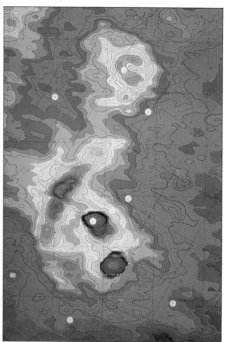
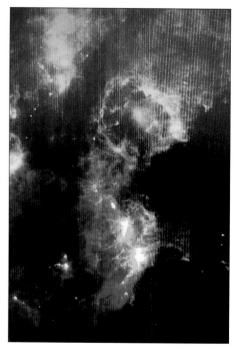

Broadcasting the news

Television and radio are the most powerful means of mass-communication in existence. Television in particular can present images and ideas to millions of people at the same time. It has been estimated that 2,500 million people watched the 23rd Olympic Games in Los Angeles, USA, on television in 1984. Almost one third of the world's population – 1,600 million people – watched the Live Aid pop concert in 1985.

Broadcasting is entering a period of great change. **Satellite television, cable television** and television with stereo sound are already commonplace in many countries. During the 1990s, new technology will literally change the shape of our television sets.

In the late 1990s, television sets with wide, letterbox-shaped screens will go on sale in Europe. At the moment, television pictures are made up of 625 horizontal lines (525 in Japan and the USA). The new widescreen sets will produce pictures with double this number of lines. The pictures will be four times clearer than today's television pictures. Japan was the first country to develop High Definition Television (HDTV). Europe is now developing its own HDTV system, in a research project called Eureka 95. The project is enormous. Forty organizations in 10 countries are involved. The first live transmission of the European HDTV system took place in 1990. The subject was the World Cup football match between Italy and Uruguay. The Eureka 95 project is timed so that the complete system will be ready for the 1992 Olympic Games in Barcelona, Spain.

The importance of HDTV goes far beyond simply providing better television pictures. The television set will be quite a powerful computer and the microchips it will use will be amongst the most advanced ever made. There will be a huge demand for them, not only from television manufacturers but also from manufacturers of a variety of military and medical equipment. The cinema industry is likely to change over to high definition video instead of film. The market for the chips is so huge that all the countries capable of making HDTV chips will be in keen competition with each other for as large a share as possible of the multi-billion dollar market that is expected.

Satellite radio?

Satellite television is already commonplace. By the end of the 1990s, satellite radio may be just as common. Motorists in particular will benefit from this development. In one demonstration, a simulated satellite radio transmitter was placed on top of the Jura mountains in Switzerland. Its transmissions were picked up clearly by a car fitted with a suitable receiver. When the car entered a tunnel, the normal radio broadcast faded away, but the satellite broadcast came through loud and clear all the way through the tunnel! The reason is that the satellite radio receiver was designed to use reflections of the satellite signal bouncing off nearby obstacles. Satellite radio will therefore end the annoying radio silences that occur every time a motorist drives underneath a bridge or through a tunnel.

Watch that radio!

A radio with a screen sounds like a description of a television set, but screens are actually being added to radios to give the listener extra information and to improve reception.

Solar-powered television takes the news to a remote village in Niger.

The 1992 Olympic Games in Barcelona, Spain will be transmitted by high definition television. The sports hall (above and inset) and the stadium are part of the complex built specially for the games.

Farmers in developing countries (right, paddy fields in India) could receive printed information and advice through a radio data system. One or more villages could make use of a single radio and printer.

The Radio Data System (RDS) works by transmitting an inaudible radio signal with the programmes. All radio sets pick up the signal but only radios with the necessary decoding circuits can make use of it. They use it in several ways. The radio constantly compares the reception quality of the various frequencies of a station and automatically tunes in to the best. It will search for a particular type of programme – a pop concert, some jazz, a play or the news, for example – and if you want to be sure of hearing a programme, the radio will re-tune automatically to the correct station at the right time.

RDS has some interesting possibilities for the future. Notes for schools programmes, for example, could be transmitted by RDS and printed out by a printer connected to the radio. RDS was designed by the BBC in Britain, but it will be available in other countries too. About a dozen European countries have agreed to begin RDS services so far.

A similar system in the Third World could transmit notes giving medical or farming advice over the radio. A range of notes would be transmitted one after another. The user would simply have to say which notes were wanted by keying given code numbers into the printer unit. The next time the required notes were transmitted, they would be turned into printed text by the printer.

Newspapers on computer

Satellites are becoming increasingly important in the newspaper business. All the information that goes to make up a newspaper is fed into the newspaper's computer system. It consists of a central computer linked to dozens of desk-top terminals. Reporters enter their stories at these terminals and editors check the stories using computer terminals. The pages are then designed on a computer terminal that makes sure that all the text and photographs will fit on the pages. Advertisements are added, also by computer. When everyone is satisfied that the newspaper is ready to be printed, the same computer system even controls the making of the printing plates. A very complicated information-based system like a newspaper is ideally suited to computerization.

Getting the facts by fax

Newspapers are sometimes distributed to several printing centres in different cities or countries by satellite so that they can all be printed simultaneously and appear in the shops at the same time. In future, a new system which combines satellite distribution and fax machines could enable us to have newspapers faxed directly to our homes and offices from the publisher.

Fax machines are normally used by connecting one fax machine to one other fax machine by a telephone line and then sending a message from one to the other. Clearly, contacting thousands or millions of people in this way to fax a newspaper to each of them would take far too long. The new system broadcasts newspapers in the same way as television programmes. They are picked up by an ordinary rooftop television aerial and fed to a decoder, which changes them into a form that a fax machine can print out. A million people could be contacted and sent a newspaper by this method within a few minutes.

The same system could be used to, for example, distribute important information to all the hospitals in an area at the same time.

satellite television – television programmes that are transmitted from a ground station up to a satellite in Space and then directly to viewers' homes. This is also called Direct Broadcast by Satellite (DBS) and Direct-To-Home (DTH) satellite television.
cable television – television programmes that are delivered to the viewer's house by a metal or optical fibre cable instead of via a rooftop aerial.

In print. Modern newspaper offices are highly computerized. Once the stories are keyed in to the computer, they are edited on the screen, and not on paper.

At the cinema

Since its earliest days, the cinema has been a powerful communications medium, showing audiences views of the world that they might otherwise never see. In recent years, as the quality of television pictures and sound have improved, the film industry has had to come up with new ways of making the experience of seeing a film in the cinema more impressive than on television.

New sound and vision systems aim to make people in the audience believe that they are really in the middle of the action on the screen. One way of doing this is to surround the audience with a curved screen. The film's sound track is also directed at the audience from all angles to bring the action to life.

Some cinemas have huge screens up to 20m high wrapped around the front and sides of the audience, and also dome-shaped screens up to 27m across hanging above the audience. One system, IMAX Magic Carpet, uses two screens, one in front of the audience and one below a transparent seating deck. Films to be shown on the system are made using two cameras mounted on a special rig, with one camera pointing straight ahead and the other pointing downwards.

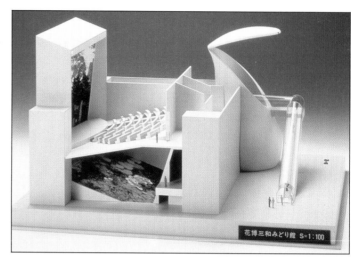

Cinema magic. Huge screens (bottom), and even two screens (above, a model) are designed to give the audience a feeling of being 'right in the picture'.

Photography

In future, photography will face increasing competition from alternative ways of recording images. Cameras can now store still pictures as digital codes on magnetic tape or a magnetic disc similar to computer memory discs. As they do not use any photographic film at all, they are sometimes called filmless cameras.

The disadvantage of the filmless camera is that it requires additional equipment to complete the system. To see the photographs, the camera must be plugged into a television set. To obtain prints of the photographs, the camera must be plugged into a printer. If the cost of the system can be reduced and the picture quality improved, the filmless camera might be more appealing. The future of photography probably lies in a combination of chemical and electronic techniques. Photographs could be recorded on photographic film and then improved in quality by computer.

Fooling the brain

However large or impressive a cinema picture is, it is shown on a flat screen. Films might seem more realistic if they could be made in 3-D (three dimensions). This can be done by feeding the viewer's left eye with a slightly different view of everything compared to what the right eye is shown. The viewer's brain combines the two images and is fooled into believing that objects in the picture are standing out from the flat screen as if they were real. Each eye must not see the image intended for the other eye. In the past this was done by making the two images two different colours and using coloured spectacles to allow only one image through to each eye. They were not popular with cinema audiences.

In future, 3-D cinema systems may use spectacles with lenses made from **liquid crystal**. The lenses are normally clear, but they can be made to turn black and prevent light from passing through by using a tiny electric current through the liquid crystal material. By switching the current to each lens in turn very rapidly and synchronizing this with the film on the screen, the left eye always sees a left eye image and the right eye always sees a right eye image. The effect of this is to give the viewer the impression of seeing a full-colour, three-dimensional image. A full-colour 3-D cinema system using cordless liquid crystal spectacles in this way was built at Expo 90 in Osaka, Japan, in 1990.

Ideally, audiences should not have to use any special eye-wear. It may be possible to do this by constructing the cinema screen from a series of fine vertical strips instead of a flat panel. Two images are projected on to the screen at the same time. They are divided into thin strips and interleaved together. A viewer's left eye sees all the strips that make up the left eye image. The right eye sees all the strips that make up the right eye image and the brain combines the two flat images into a single 3-D image. A small-screen television version of this system has already been built. It works, but only if the viewer sits in precisely the right position!

Many of these and other advanced cinema systems are the product of the IMAX Systems Corporation in Canada. There are over 70 IMAX cinemas around the world now and there will be over 100 by 1992. Most are in the USA.

> **liquid crystal** – a material made from crystals that move when they are electrified. (See glossary, page 44.)

Computer revolution

Computers have revolutionized the way we collect, store, process, transmit and display information. Without computers, we would not have the sophisticated communications networks that encircle our world. Many offices depend on computers of one sort or another.

Computers can do things that the human brain is incapable of doing. They can process huge amounts of information very quickly, but they are actually very simple adding machines. All they can do is add two numbers together, one addition at a time. Subtraction, multiplication and division can all be done by clever variations of this basic process. Some computers contain several **processors** which can divide up a problem and work on different parts of it at the same time. This is called parallel processing. It can save a great deal of time when the computer is tackling very complex problems such as weather forecasting. This is a particularly difficult job because so many different bits of information, such as temperature, air pressure, rainfall, wind speed and wind direction, change from moment to moment and they all affect each other.

The Cray-2 computer, for example, can divide up a problem between up to four 'background

A Cray-2 supercomputer at a NASA research centre in California, USA. The circuit boards are bathed in a cooling liquid to prevent them from heating up and melting the machine!

processors' under the control of the master processor. The Cray-2 is one of the most powerful computers in the world. It can carry out up to 1,200 million calculations every second. Supercomputers like the Cray-2 are used to solve the most complicated problems.

Expert systems

People at work often need to discuss a problem with an expert. A doctor might want to check his

Taking the train. Buying a railway ticket in India (left) can take a very long time, but computers have speeded up the process in New Delhi.

Computers of the future (right) may combine electronic machines with biological cells. This picture, taken through a microscope, shows human nerve cells growing on a computer chip. Hybrid computers (which combine living nerve cells and computer chips) could be one billion times more powerful than a silicon computer of the same size. They could handle very complex tasks such as robot vision.

An inside view

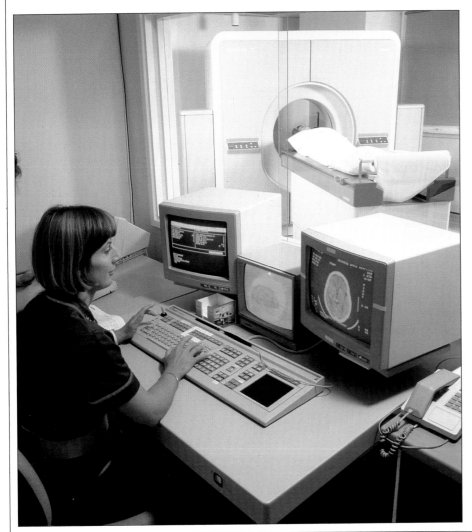

A technique called computerized tomography (CT) gives doctors a new kind of X-ray picture. A CT scan involves taking X-rays of a patient from a series of different angles. All the X-ray reflections from inside the body are collected and added together by a computer to produce a picture that looks like a slice through the body.

Other techniques are being developed that use less harmful kinds of **radiation**. One system, called chronocoherent imaging, uses intense beams of light from lasers to form detailed images of what lies beneath the skin. All these techniques rely on computers to organize the information in a useful way.

A CT scanner takes X-rays of the patient's head and the computer uses the data to show a cross-section of the patient's brain.

or her thoughts on a patient's illness with a more experienced doctor. A power station controller may want to talk to the designer of one of the station's control systems to check that it is operating correctly and safely. A motor mechanic may want to ask a car manufacturer about how a particular part of an engine should be repaired. In all these cases, the expert knowledge of the more experienced person or specialist organization can be stored in a computer. The less experienced person can then ask the computer for the expert's advice by answering a series of questions presented on the computer screen. This is called an expert system.

Computer copies of the brain

One branch of computer research is concentrating on designing computers that will tackle problems in a similar way to a human brain. Computers like this are called artificial **neural** networks, or ANNs. If ANNs can be made to work as their designers wish, they will revolutionize computers and the way we use them. They will be much better at carrying out the tasks that people do well and today's computers do very badly. The most important of these is pattern recognition. We understand much of what we see and hear by recognizing patterns in the sounds and images. ANN-based computers will be very important in the design of the vision and hearing systems of intelligent robots. Some computer experts have predicted that computer power could catch up with the power of the human brain by the year 2015.

Computers see the light

Looking further into the future, optical computers promise exciting advances. An optical computer uses light beams instead of wires to transmit information which will travel along optical fibres at the speed of light. Optical computers are expected to operate at speeds undreamt of today, perhaps 1000 times faster than existing computers.

Optical computers will make telephone systems more efficient and allow videophones to be developed (see page 16). Voice recognition systems would also benefit from the optical computer's speed and huge information processing capacity. If optical communications and voice recognition were combined, a future telephone would be able to produce a printed copy of a conversation as it actually happened. Switching in a translation system would enable copies of the conversation to be printed in different languages. If it sounds like science fiction to you, prototype optical computers have already been built! They are at the same stage in development as electronic computers were perhaps 30 years ago, but they are advancing rapidly.

Fractal geometry

Computers are very good at drawing straight lines and perfect curves, but until recently they could not copy the very crinkly, complex patterns of the real world. In 1984 Benoit Mandelbrot invented fractals. Fractals are mathematical equations which allow the computer to produce images of the real world. These images are realistic enough for scientists to use to predict what might happen in particular situations — what might happen if the course of a river is altered, how air pollution from a factory might spread, how a coastline might be eroded over several decades, and so on.

Created by computer. Fractals produce intricate patterns that reveal more and more detail, however much they are magnified.

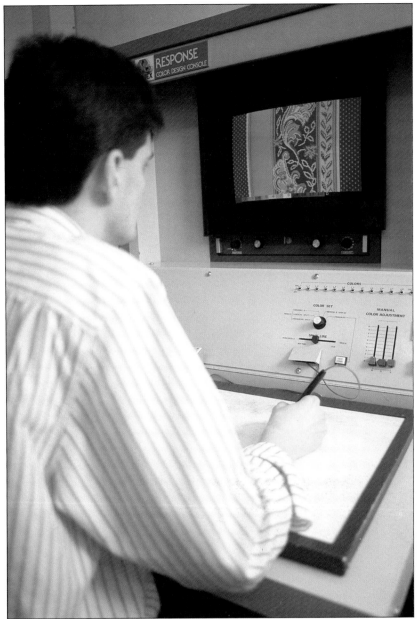

桃 花 船
桃花辮 漂 水 面，
变 成 许 多 桃 花 船。
桃 花 船 真 美 丽，
蚂 蚁 坐 上 去 游 玩。

A computer with a stylus can be used to design fabrics (left), or to write text in a language that has too many characters to go on a keyboard (above).

The Chinese poem says:
The petals of the peach float on the water.
Each petal becomes a peach blossom boat.
Peach blossom boats are very beautiful.
An insect rides on the boats for fun.

The listening computer?

Many people are put off using a computer because of the difficulty of communicating with it. The only way of communicating with most computers is by typing instructions on a keyboard. Keyboards are big and noisy, and they tend to get in the way when people come together for a meeting. A computer that can understand speech would be more 'user-friendly' and acceptable. Optical computers which understand human speech may be a little way off in the future, but other ways of making it easier to communicate with a computer are here already. Computers that understand handwriting are already available. Words written on the surface of the computer with a special **stylus** are converted directly into text in the computer's memory. Without the need for a keyboard, the computer can be made much smaller and flatter.

This type of 'stylus' computer is needed more urgently in the Far East than in Europe or the United States, because of the type of languages used in the Far East. They are based on thousands of pictorial characters instead of our own alphabet of only 26 letters, so it is difficult to build a keyboard of a practical size. Some stylus computers get better at reading their user's handwriting because they learn how their users write different letters and numbers. Another advantage of the stylus computer is that without a keyboard it can be made more resistant to the effects of dust, dirt, heat and chemicals. It can therefore be used in situations where a normal computer would be severely damaged, for example on a building site.

Creating new worlds

Computers are very good at processing words and doing arithmetic. Pictures are more difficult for computers to work with because pictures contain an astonishing amount of information. All the words in this book are roughly equivalent to about 700,000 bits of information. It was written using a small personal computer which can easily store and process that amount of information. By contrast, a single colour picture in this book is equivalent to tens of *millions* of bits of information. This huge amount of information can only be stored and processed quickly by the most powerful computers.

Less powerful computers can store and display simpler, less detailed pictures with fewer colours. These computers are used to produce the images for video games systems (see pages 9–10). If the images do not have to be created and changed very quickly, a small computer can build up a very detailed image over several seconds, minutes or even hours. If a sequence of images created in this way is recorded on video tape and the tape is played, the result is computer-generated 'animation'. This is often used to advertise products on television or to produce backgrounds or scenes for films.

Flight simulators use computer images. These machines are used to train airline and military pilots. The crew sits in an aircraft cockpit and through the windows they see a view of the airport around them. As their aircraft thunders down the runway and takes off, it tips up and they see the ground disappear below them as they rise into the air. Actually, they never leave the ground! The view through the cockpit windows is created by a computer and projected on to screens all around the cockpit. It has to look real and change precisely in time with the pilot's control movements. The view can also be changed by the computers to simulate night or day, and stormy or foggy conditions.

Flight simulators are important for two reasons. They enable flight crews to practise what they should do in dangerous situations over and over again without risking their lives in a real aircraft. Secondly, they enable the crew to be trained without taking airliners out of passenger service. Simulators are also used to train people who monitor and control complex machines and systems such as nuclear power stations and traffic control systems.

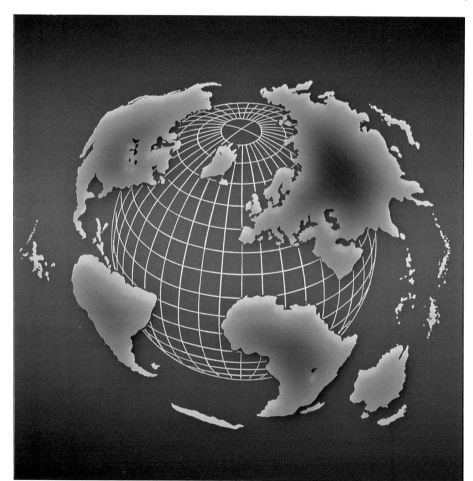

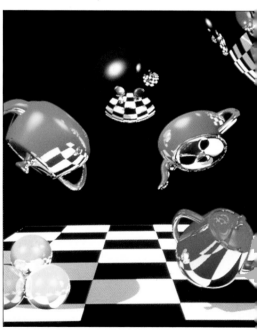

Computer graphics can be used for fun (above), but they can also be used to create more useful images (left), for study and training.

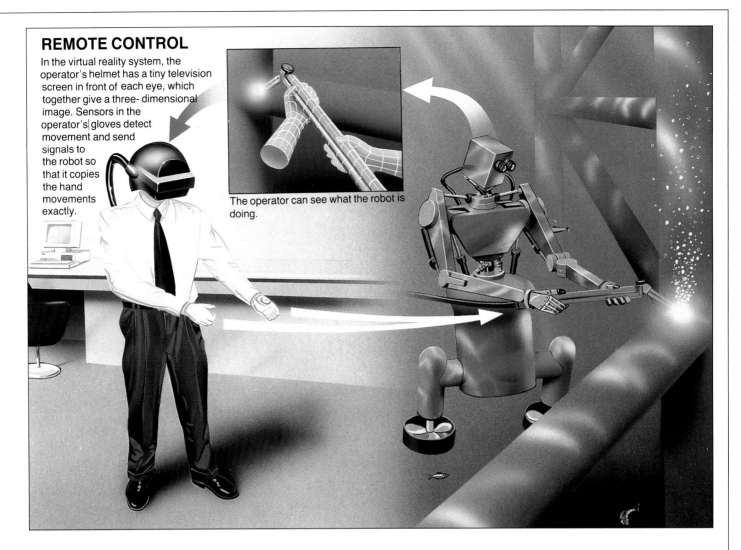

REMOTE CONTROL

In the virtual reality system, the operator's helmet has a tiny television screen in front of each eye, which together give a three-dimensional image. Sensors in the operator's gloves detect movement and send signals to the robot so that it copies the hand movements exactly.

The operator can see what the robot is doing.

Reality . . . or is it?

The ability to create an artificial world, using an extraordinary technique called virtual reality, will be very important in the future. As robots become more advanced and are able to do more jobs, they are likely to be used in dangerous environments such as in Space, under the sea or in high radiation areas of nuclear reactors. The ideal robot would be able to move, see and hear, but under the control of a human brain, because the human brain is still the most powerful computer that we have. It may not be able to do millions of calculations per second, but it can solve a greater variety of problems in the real world more effectively than any computer.

In a virtual reality system, everything the robot sees and hears is relayed to a hemlet worn by its operator. Everything the robot sees with its television camera eyes is projected on to the inside of the helmet visor in front of the operator's eyes. If the operator turns to one side, sensors on his or her suit detect this and relay it to the robot so that it, too, turns. If the

operator stretches out a hand to pick up something that appears in the visor, the robot's hand stretches out and actually picks up the object. Virtual reality system robots may be used to service Space stations in this way. They could carry out tasks outside the station, under the control of human operators safely cocooned inside. The system depends on reliable two-way radio communications of images and control signals between the operator and robot.

processor – the part of a computer that does all the arithmetic and also controls other parts of the computer.
radiation – energy given out by something. It may be in the form of radiowaves, heat, light particles or sound.
neural – describing anything to do with nerves, the fibres that carry electrical signals between the brain and the rest of the body.
stylus – a pointed instrument used to trace letters or shapes on a soft pad.

The Earth from Space

The ability to communicate with satellites carrying cameras pointed at the Earth has led to a very important branch of science called remote sensing. It is important because it gives us valuable information about the Earth's weather, its natural resources and its plant life.

Most satellites orbit the Earth around the equator, but remote sensing satellites orbit from pole to pole. As the satellite orbits in a north-south direction while the planet revolves below it, every part of the planet eventually passes beneath the satellite. For example, one remote sensing satellite called Landsat 5 sees every part of the Earth once in every 233 orbits.

Different types of rocks and soil, healthy plants and diseased plants each reflect the Sun's radiation differently. Our eyes are sensitive to only a tiny fraction of the Sun's radiation which we call light. The sensors used by remote sensing satellites are sensitive to a much wider range of **wavelengths**. By tuning in to different wavelengths, remote sensing satellites can be programmed to search for valuable minerals, to monitor crops or forests for diseases or to look for the effects of drought. They can show up the effects of pollution in the sea or rivers and observe the movements of icebergs in the sea, which is of great interest to shipping. The destruction of the world's rainforests can also be seen clearly in satellite photographs.

The satellite's measurements are transmitted to Earth by radio and used to create pictures. Optical (visible light) pictures show the Earth as we would see it if we looked down at it from a great height. Other pictures of, for example, the ground or the ocean, show different temperatures in different colours. As these colours do not really exist, they are called artificial colours or false colours.

Studying the atmosphere

Remote sensing satellites can look at the atmosphere as well as the Earth's surface. NASA's Upper Atmosphere Research Satellite (UARS) will measure chemicals in the atmosphere. It is due to be launched by the Space shuttle Atlantis in 1991. The satellite, weighing six tonnes and measuring 19m, should improve our knowledge of the upper atmosphere, including the ozone layer. This is a part of the atmosphere that scientists are very concerned about. Some of the chemicals that we use in spray cans and refrigerators can damage the ozone layer, allowing more of the Sun's harmful radiation to reach the Earth's surface.

Benefits to the Third World

Remote sensing by satellite was the result of military research. It was later used for making maps and looking for valuable minerals. Now and in future it will benefit developing countries too. Weather satellites can warn of the approach of a violent storm or hurricane. If a country suffers a disaster such as a flood, satellite images quickly reveal which parts of the country are flooded and which are not. This helps the rescue services to plan where to concentrate their efforts without having to waste time surveying the land from

With global warming in mind. After its launch in 1991, the European Remote-sensing Satellite (ERS-1) (above, undergoing final ground tests in France) will be used to study the oceans and investigate climate change (right).

ground level or from aircraft. Satellite images can also show how dry the land is and whether or not the plants on it are alive or dead. This helps relief workers to follow the course of drought conditions and send emergency food supplies to the worst affected areas shown by the satellite photographs.

Some remote sensing satellites have radar systems. These transmit radio waves down to the ground and measure the reflections that return to the spacecraft. Radio waves can pass through the top few metres of soil and show what is underneath it. By studying the shape of the rock under the soil or sandy surface layers, scientists can sometimes discover new underground water supplies. This is clearly important in very dry countries.

> **wavelength** – Light, radio waves and X-rays are all different parts of the electromagnetic spectrum. They consist of electrical and magnetic vibrations. The distance between two vibrations that are next to each other is called the wavelength.

A new look at Death Valley in California, USA (above). This Landsat satellite image of Death Valley reveals which areas might be worth exploring for minerals. Here, ground containing clay shows up as red, iron oxide as green and areas containing both as yellowish. White indicates an area of little geological interest.

Weather watch. A picture from Skylab shows a typhoon developing. Such pictures give advance warnings of severe weather.

Rainforests on fire

Landsat photographs are a good way of monitoring what is happening on the Earth, especially in areas that are difficult to explore on the ground. The picture (left) shows dense forest vegetation in Brazil, coloured red. The neat white lines are roads cut into the forest to allow poor farmers to clear land for growing crops. The picture (bottom left), taken five years later, shows how much forest has been destroyed by cutting and burning the trees. The soil does not remain fertile for long, so farmers will be forced to clear more forest every few years.

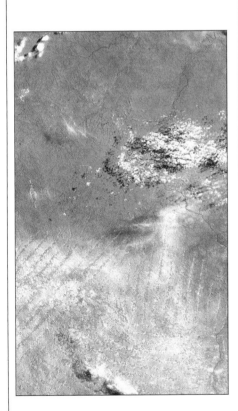

Tracking and tagging

By monitoring the movements of an animal or a group of animals, scientists can often discover more about the animal's breeding and feeding behaviour. The way the animals use the land they live on may also be revealed by monitoring their movements.

In the past, the only way to do this was to follow the animals around and watch their movements. When small, lightweight radio transmitters became available they were fitted to collars worn by the animals. Scientists could monitor their movements from up to several kilometres away, using mobile radio receivers. In many studies, this system is still used, but the Space Age has given scientists a much more convenient system for long-range animal tracking. Animals in one country can be tracked from the comfort of an office or laboratory in another country.

The animal wears a collar carrying a radio transmitter. Signals from the transmitter are picked up by satellites orbiting the Earth. The satellites relay the signals back down to the receivers on the ground, where the animal's position can be recorded.

A project designed to monitor the movements of elephants in Kenya uses such a system. Several wild elephants were fitted with battery-powered radio collars. Radio signals transmitted from the collars are relayed by satellite to a ground station in France and from there to the elephant house at London Zoo. There, the elephants' movements are transferred on to a map of the area. The aim of the project is to find out the best way of managing the land so that elephants and people can live in the same area without one threatening the other. Elephants often roam on to farmland and damage buildings and crops, so farmers and their families suffer. Poachers kill elephants because of the huge amounts of money they can make from selling the ivory tusks. In 1981, over 40,000 elephants lived in the Tsavo National Park, one of Kenya's wildlife parks. By the end of the 1980s, less than 4,000 were left.

Satellite tracking will provide detailed information about the animals' movements, so that both elephants and farmland can be better protected in future.

Crime watch

Electronic tagging has also been used to reduce overcrowding in prisons. In some countries, people who have committed minor crimes have been tagged instead of being sent to prison. To monitor the movements of offenders and ensure that they stay within an approved area, an electronic tag is strapped to one ankle. It transmits a radio signal to a receiver in the person's home. If the person moves too far away from the receiver, the signal from the tag becomes too weak for the receiver to detect it. An alarm signal is automatically sent to a central monitoring station.

Elephants in Kenya, Africa, are being tracked by satellite. Their movements are relayed to a computer at London Zoo, England, and shown on a map (right).

Design problems. Tracking animals means having equipment suitable for each species. The big cats have narrow heads and the collars holding the transmitter may slip off. Whales (far left) need waterproof equipment. Polar bears (left) tend to chew their collars. Elephants may crush the equipment against a tree. Engineers have to solve these problems if the tracking projects are to be successful.

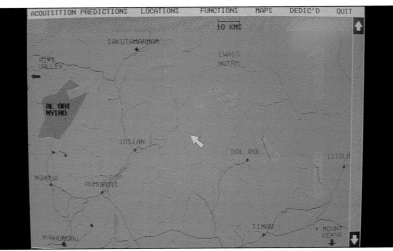

Communications: the key to success?

Some countries look upon advanced communications systems as their key to a successful future in a very competitive business world. Singapore is one of those countries. It has built one of the world's most advanced Integrated Services Digital Networks, the system that allows telephone messages and computer data to be sent together through the same network.

The port of Singapore shows how the system can be used to advantage. As ships arrive at the port, details of their cargoes are sent ahead by telephone, fax or telex. By the time each ship requests permission to dock, the port's computer system knows the position of every cargo container on the ship and where it is going. Using this information, the computer works out the best way to unload the cargo without unbalancing the ship. This has cut the unloading time from an average of two days to just a few hours. More ships can therefore be docked, unloaded, loaded again with different cargoes and sent on their way, increasing the port's income.

People bringing goods into Singapore have to apply for permission to do so. This used to require dozens of forms, covering different types of goods. It usually took several days to get the necessary permissions. The computerized system completes the process in a few minutes. This means that goods can be cleared from the dockside in the minimum time, making room for new goods coming in.

The port's computer system is part of a computer network called Tradenet. There are other networks aimed at other businesses and services – one for the legal profession, another for doctors and hospitals, yet another for schools and so on. The whole community is linking up through computers and communications. It does not simply make business more efficient and profitable. It also improves the quality of life for the people in Singapore. For example, all the stations of Singapore's underground train system are monitored by computers and all the computers are all linked together via the ISDN.

The computer system knows how many tickets are bought for which journeys and when. If the number of people who want to travel by train exceeds a certain level, more trains are automatically called into service to prevent overcrowding.

Data for discussion
● Imagine living in a country like Singapore, where an ISDN system was in operation. How might your daily life and that of your family be improved by the system? Would there be any disadvantages for anybody?

Machines take over. Computer systems are used to help organize business affairs, transport, education and other aspects of life in Singapore (below and right).

Conclusions

ISDN is the communications technology of the future. It will not only revolutionize international trade and business, it will also begin to change our everyday lives. The telephone will become a doorway into a multitude of new information and communication services.

The countries that will take up the new technology are likely to be countries which already have quite advanced communications networks. Third World countries are unlikely to be able to afford the immense cost of building or buying these new systems. ISDN seems likely, therefore, to widen the gap between developed and developing countries.

On the other hand, some new communications technologies *will* benefit Third World countries. Mobile satellite communications in particular will enable people to bypass an unreliable telephone system and reach outlying rural districts. Satellites will play a more important role in monitoring developing countries for the first signs of natural disasters and also in studying longer-term problems such as the spread of pests and diseases through food crops. As developed countries become more aware of the damage that is being done to the world around us by, amongst other things, the poisonous waste materials poured out by some industries, the use of chemicals that damage the atmosphere and the clearance of the equatorial rainforests, information collection and communication systems will increasingly be used to identify problem areas so that action can be taken. We will all benefit from this.

Glossary

analogue – an analogue signal is an electrical copy of the original information. An analogue telephone line carries an electrical signal that varies in step with the voice that produced it. Compare this with **digital.**

bus – in electronics, a bus is a pathway for information.

cable television – television programmes that are delivered to the viewer's house by a metal or optical fibre cable instead of via a rooftop aerial.

CD – Compact Disc. A mirror-like disc used for making high-quality recordings of music.

CD-ROM – Compact Disc Read-Only Memory. This is a laser disc used to store computer data instead of music. The data recorded on it cannot be wiped or erased and new data recorded. It is therefore a 'read only' information storage device.

data – information, especially information in a form that can be processed by a computer.

digital – a digital signal consists of a stream of electrical pulses, all the same size. The pattern, or code, of the pulses carries the information. Compare this with **analogue.**

electromagnetic waves – Waves of energy composed of vibrating electric and magnetic fields. Light, radio and X-rays are examples of electromagnetic waves.

fibre optic cable – a cable made from a bundle of fine glass strands. Information is transmitted along the cable in the form of an intense beam of light.

high definition television – a television broadcasting system capable of creating pictures of much better quality than we have today. Definition refers to the smallness of detail that can be shown by the screen. High definition means finely detailed.

infra-red – energy that lies between visible light and radio waves, just beyond the red end of the rainbow.

liquid crystal – A material made from crystals that move when they are electrified. The material is normally clear, but when electrified, the crystals move so as to stop light passing through. Liquid crystal watch and calculator displays and television screens work in this way.

navigation – finding a safe route from one place to another place, especially by ship or aircraft.

network – a system of interconnected equipment such as radio sets, telephones or computers that can communicate with each other.

neural – describing anything to do with nerves, the fibres that carry electrical signals between the brain and the rest of the body.

passwords – passwords are words or numbers known only to people who are allowed to operate a system. The system will not operate until it receives the correct passwords.

processor – the part of a computer that does all the arithmetic and also controls other parts of the computer.

radiation – energy given out by something. It may be in the form of radio waves, heat, light particles or sound.

satellites – unmanned spacecraft in orbit around a planet.

satellite television – television programmes that are transmitted from a ground station up to a satellite in Space and then directly to viewers' homes. This is also called Direct Broadcast by Satellite (DBS) and Direct-To-Home (DTH) satellite television.

synchronized – linked in time so that the operation of one thing is kept in step with the operation of another.

technology – the application of science to solving practical problems.

telecommunications – communications by telephone, radio or television.

wavelength – light, radio waves and X-rays are all different parts of the electromagnetic spectrum. They consist of electrical and magnetic vibrations. The distance between two vibrations that are next to each other is called the wavelength.

X-rays – radiation given out when particles called electrons are made to move very fast and then brought to rest very quickly. They can pass through soft material such as skin easily, less easily through heavier materials such as bone.